Side Effects

Poems

Patricia Wixon

First U.S. edition 2014

Editor and Publisher: Laura LeHew

Proofreaders: Harriot West
                         Nancy Carol Moody
                         Karen Locke
                         Roy R. Seitz

Cover photo Angels Landing, Zion National Park © R. Eric Stone
    www.rericstone.com

www.utteredchaos.org

ISBN 978-0-9889366-3-8

In memory of my parents
Orlo Harrison Maughan and Halcyon Delight Maughan

and for Vince

Everything is biographical...what we make, why we make it, what we are drawn to, everything is collage.
—Michael Ondaatje

Contents

Metamorphosis

This story might be about rain pressing dirt
around redwood roots spreading counterweights
for a trunk stretching up half a millennium,
half the life of the grove
and later more rain washing, winding a path,
and when the tree thunders down
declaring its death, a seed burrows,
shoots red roots, more.

This story might be of hunters climbing
in caves, their flashlights scanning for nests,
balls of glass built by swiftlets
winding and stringing their sticky saliva
to hang homes in the dark—no twigs,
no grass—just spittle dried hard,
right for eggs. And this is about skilled hunters
who snap off nests for soup.

This story will start with a word that moves
mouth to mouth, morphing until someone draws
letters on a page in a particular shape
to keep the story whole. The first letter
will be embellished, illuminated as in *The Book
of Hours* to stay there even as air devours half
the paper's life, then more, until nothing's left
but a tarnished *T* holding the story's memory.

In Canyons of the Ancients: Lowry Pueblo

Winds of the Great Sage Plain blast sand
against our backs as we bend through the opening
without a door. Stacked red rock leads us to the kiva

whose circling wall holds flecks of white plaster
smoothed for murals eight hundred years ago.
Missing parts, dark painted blocks interlocked

like Legos, live only in photos excavators took.
Had ancestral painters mimicked their world—
sandstone layers hanging over cliffs, slab caves,

cracks shimmed with colored pebbles, grass, dirt,
and urine? Are these square clouds prayers
to seasons battering this hill?

We move back out onto the vista point,
stand in wind and search the sky for prayers.

Gray Spring

The spring she moved to the old house
and watched clouds fall to mist

over flat acres of gray-brown rhizomes,
sun rarely shone—not at dawn or

settling dusk or any time of day.
No rainbows or cutting through

with slanted shafts of light like paintings
on Sunday School walls.

Gray day after day made her certain
she didn't want to stay where her world view

was squeezed to acres of lopped brown stalks
rigid in the rain. Then late that spring

she found green specks dotting clumps of dirt,
watched tiny spears break through clods,

grow twice their height each day.
Suddenly a first bud opened, translucent tissue

petals—brilliant yellow, amber beard—
holding the sun.

Stitches at the Museum

Song Dynasty
This silk brocade with shapes of deep maroon and blue,
cream and green, interwoven with threads of gold,
a heavy fabric woven for long skirts, sleeve panels,
and baby wraps to secure each bundled child. Think of women
braiding buttons of knotted silk, working slender needles
for intricacies eight hundred years ago.

Renaissance
French women stitched this fine muslin—tiny fancy pleats
and lace collars as wide as dinner plates.
Threads holding necklines and sleeves move in and out
so identical in length it's hard to believe they were sewn
by hand. Ribbons and lace trim on a dress that might
never have been laundered but worn to disintegration.

Nez Perce
The woman stitching rows of trade beads on this martingale
worked it as carefully for her horse as for her dress—
leather tanned with urine and cut to fit with few seams,
few holes to force lacing through. Berry-dyed in narrow strips
to outline seams. and beads strung on a single strand,
secured at intervals with carefully hidden thread.

Midwest Depression
Farm wives made do tearing worn-out clothes into rags, saving
parts still good—backs of pockets, inside yokes, an upper piece
of sleeve. Sewing tiny seams, they turned triangles into squares, then
blocks and rows, top layers stacked and stitched with heavy thread
that puckered when the needle pulled too tight, named their work
Midnight Star, Garden of Eden, December Rose.

Georgia's View

On Chimney Rock Trail a mile high
behind Ghost Ranch, thin clouds gather,
temperature so perfect I can't feel the air.

Scattered rocks and footprints in silt
after yesterday's brief shower. Part way up
the edge lets go. Another piece of desert varnish

drops among stones piling the ravine floor.
A black dot becomes a crow, then another screaming
a caw caw cawphony—a raw round

echoing against the chimney's sharp slabs.
I turn to face Georgia O'Keeffe's favored view:
sun on Pedernal,

evenly rounded hills at its base—all in the right
colors: dry clay red, dark foggy blue,
intermittent angles of white.

To the Women at Fort Vancouver, 1824

Arriving that rainy winter, you were prepared
to accept your place at dinner
separate from Hudson's Bay Company men

unless your husband was pastor, then you'd sit
with officials. No matter where you ate you took care
to remain a lady, cheeks powdered

with vermilion, hemmed skirts ankle-high
so rain wouldn't pull them to mud.
You strung laundry to dry leaving space

to stoke the fire for boiling water, porridge, stew.
For more than a century, Fort records noted each man
and later when archaeologists began to dig,

they attributed all artifacts to men—recorded tiny lils
screened from Stratum 3 as used to pin men's ruffs,
not knowing lils were brought by you

for veils at special times. Notes left out you
who tended the men and children—washed, starched,
pieced blankets from clothes too worn to mend.

After you were gone, did everything you'd touched
dissolve to earth? As scientists sifted, did they toss aside
your fragments, miss traces of you altogether?

Fourth Grade Oregon History

They studied who was here years before great-grandfathers
homesteaded and found gold turning hills into wheat.

They chanted tribe names: Siletz, Chinook, Modoc, Nez Perce,
rolled their tongues on Coquille, Kalapuya, Molalla,

imagined who picked bearberries or golden currants,
who ground acorns for mush, wove red cedar baskets.

They learned whole families marched hundreds of miles—
children walking the whole way, babies born on the trail—

forced to live on reservations with nothing familiar
around them, not even food.

The class divided into teams named Eagle king of the air,
Wolf genius of land, Whale lord of the sea, and Frog

linker of land and sea. One group named themselves Owl
for the newly fledged owlets in their barns.

Teams gouged and carved the sugar pine log, watched birds
and animals emerge perched on shoulders like acrobats.

When their totem was done, the post digger came, then the lifter,
and the man with cement to plant it by the school's front door.

On the second night, as Hawk watched Moon slide by Beaver,
three teen-agers jumped from a pickup, set their chainsaw

spinning its lethal whirl. Eagle and Owl flew off with their souls,
while Beaver and the others thundered to the ground.

First Anniversary, February 12, 1933

Here's a photo of a couple
where the sharpest line
defines the ground,
where a blurred bank of clouds
blocks a house,
a hill, a tree.
They have stepped outside
for better light.
He wears a tie, white shirt,
the knees of his suit pants show wear.
Her soft print dress drapes
from an open neck, a fine chain
and pendant at the curve.
Cap sleeves suggest she came from
a warm room, not stopping for a wrap
but galoshes, flaps hanging open,
unclasped.
They stand in snow
that mounds around his leather shoes,
she leaning slightly against his arm.
Both look directly into the camera
as if caught by the lens
of Dorothea Lange
at the edge
of the Great Depression.

Her First Job, 1939

Ruth was ready to interview for a job
advertised for a man.

Her degree in Personnel Management—
only woman in her class—gave her confidence

to take the bus to Harlem and walk six blocks,
a speck between stacked buildings blanketing the sky.

She wore her tailored suit, proper gloves,
close brown cloche—her wild red hair tucked in.

As she strode down the potholed road, heavy bare-armed
women leaned out their third story windows calling

What's that white girl doing on this street?
Don't know, but she sure looks good.

The pencil factory boss hired Ruth and used her ideas
to save company time and yellow paint.

Each day she rode the bus, walked the blocks,
heard women call out

Here she comes. Just look at that red hat.
Lady, I like the yellow one better, one you wore yesterday.

She'd smile and wave.

Aunt Edna's Painting

In this watercolor, maples have turned the air gold,
dissolved grass into shades of yellow, hills rusty brown

edged by firs holding a steady deep green though this time
of year surely many of their needles would have dropped.

Fields look soft but their color suggests stubble that crackled
as you walked and if you stumbled on a clod, stabbed your skin.

Aunt Edna doesn't show the barn, weathered brown,
five-stories tall, a thousand chickens on each floor.

A neighbor boy gathered eggs and I sometimes helped, too.
He pushed open the creaking door, chickens flapped, feathers

flew, dust filled my throat. Some chickens sat dead-still
as if I couldn't see them nesting. When I shoved my hand

beneath for eggs, their feathers felt heavy, warm.
I had to be quick or that beak drew blood. I had to be gentle

piling eggs until the bucket rounded full, ready for Granddad
to carry to the cooling shed where the neighbor lady perched

on a tall stool, her body stiff, mechanical, as she candled eggs—
pinched it between her thumb and finger for a light bulb to turn

the shell transparent. Moving one hand, she settled each egg
onto a lumpy egg sheet separating small or large or double yolks,

or ones with the dark spot of a chick.

Presence of Absence

In Syntagna Square, tourists gather on the hour to watch
the changing of the guard, each marcher silent in his white tights,
white skirt and shirt, red shoes he kicks above his head
with every step. Behind, a marble carving of an ancient soldier
on his death stone, Athens' memorial to its nameless warriors.

In Oregon, near Gold Hill, on the left fork of Sardine Creek
there's an invisible sphere, half above, half below ground
with a force that makes compasses falter, warns wild animals
not to cross. Tourists park where the sign points to VORTEX
and Native Americans skirt the forbidden ground.

That year at our dinner table where talk was always lively,
family members in their right places: baby in her high chair,
other kids down both sides, armed chairs for a parent
at each end. No one said a word about our father's empty place
the night he died, and every day thereafter.

I heard my neighbor on his deck beneath the trellis
where petunias hung from pots. He stood in the dark
year after year hacking his first smoke of the day.
When he no longer had his habit, I could hear that space.

Lifting the earthy hand built bowl, I feel a thumbprint
the potter left pressed five hundred years ago
and know he's still inside the clay.

On Steptoe Butte

It was a hot day for our sixth grade field trip
to the top of the quartzite butte standing in fields
of ripening wheat. Before we left the school bus,

our teacher explained what we wouldn't see:
how the ocean floor raised up, and sandstone
and granite wore into sedimentary soil.

We looked out windows and imagined U.S. troops
staged here for the Battle of Tohotonimme,
the price soldiers paid for crossing tribal lands.

We trudged up the road, sweating, kicking rocks
in the dust. At the top, just a pit with rotted wood walls
fallen in, granite chunks haphazardly stacked,

and a gray mouse scrambling for cover.
Robert pounced, caught its leg and tail and swung it
around and around overhead.

We girls shrieked *Stop!*—a shocked Greek chorus—
and Robert stopped, then whipped out his pocket knife
and slit the mouse throat to tail.

The air turned red
and we ran crying back to the bus,
hating Robert and farm boys everywhere.

Panorama Trail

We step off the pavement onto red dirt:
Panorama Trail edging Escalante
where air holds hot and dry.
A jackrabbit interrupts the static view,
his transparent ears upright,
their map of veins visible
as he leaps in long zigzag thrusts.

Now a Red-tailed Hawk swings high,
freezing the hare until the shadow
flies away. Deep silence in this desert Eden
where silt smothers footfalls.

The trail guide says this hike
will take us into slot canyons,
past gray-white columns and red rock
fins with seams of sandy shale
sifting away perpetually
as if the mountains were breathing—
each breath blowing off another part.
We listen for the exhale,
our own breathing distant,
our legs not our own.

Fishing the Clearwater

He hails from Idaho, likes to fish
the Clearwater, tie on a bucktail caddis
and cast by the snag on the second bend
past the Old Highway Y.

Rainbow are twelve inches here,
sheltered by drowning trees—
tops down, roots reaching up
to fan the granite slide below.

When noon rolls around he reels in,
hunches down to share rock heat,
tosses bits of sandwich crust
to tease out trout where water laps.

He'll take only six fish before he pulls off
his waders worn since the '40s—
dried fish oil stiff all these years—
and head on home to fry.

Holding On to Guilt

I walked a path narrowed tight
with brush and thick trees—
an ominous umbrella as I trailed
Father's steps. When sun
touched a clearing with white flowers
opened wide upon pointed leaves,
I picked one, pressed it to his hand.
Ah, you mustn't pick trillium, he said.
That plant will never bloom again.

Today sitting in Josef's restaurant
where sunlit flowers stand
in a vase, I recognized the sharp-edged leaves
holding white petals flat.
When he filled our glasses, I asked.
Trillium from my patch, he beamed,
enough for every table—
proud of his hold on nature.

Lessons from You, Father

It was July when you closed the front door
carrying your fishing rod and creel, angled hat
banded with dry flies, eager to fly to the mountain
lake. Soon you'd be edging your way out in waders
so glazed with fish oil they could stand alone.

That night you'd fight to stay alive, not burned
and broken like your copilot, but in shock
as your organs consumed each other. You told
the medic what to give each child. For me,
your bamboo pole, but it had already turned to ash.

In those childhood years, you'd bring home a creel
of cutthroat and fry their pink skins crisp.
Sometimes we'd peel sheets of sunburn from your
back, work to sunset in our Victory Garden,
help save tin foil wrappers for the War.

Now I cast a fly at a glint between the rocks, hear
your lessons as I watch the shadows, feel when
a strike sends line singing, feed, wind back a steady
take up. Leaves floating on the water collapse
like ash, linger, then slip beneath the surface.

Delight's Night Salvation

After those summer deaths: her father, mother,
oldest child—only ten—and then her husband Orlo

with the baby still so young. *Nothing like a 4-month-old*
to keep you going, she said.

When all the children were in bed, she'd take a piece
of chocolate hidden in her underwear drawer

let it melt on her tongue to keep her eyes open
to grade student papers, then fall asleep

soon as her head touched the pillow—and never dream.
Too tired to dream, she said, *and that's the Lord's blessing.*

Twelve Pearl Buttons

for Marvin Bell

As he reads, his palm
catches a word, rolls it

out and points. We see
Miss Dickinson's bright

white dress, her fingers
twisting closed a row

of twelve pearl buttons.
He's pulled Emily here,

opened the mystery
of her early morning walks,

her footfalls soft
barefooted,

carrying her shoes,
following her troubled dreams.

Inheritance

1
Martha's long white cloth and matching napkins
aged yellow and tawny-streaked, waiting in tissue fragments
in a box rubbed soft inside the trunk. No occasion arrived
fine enough for them to leave the dark.
Now laundered white again, the cloth spreads over our table
with all its leaves open for a family wedding.

2
Ninety years ago, one end of the oak hutch had rounded glass
and hand-crafted shelves for showing fine porcelain.
Elma preferred a secretary with a lid to fold closed when the day
became too much. Her son obliged, sawed off the end, threw
carved pieces in the wood bin. Now we ease down the drop-lid
on hinges that still hold, file envelopes in open slots.

3
Heat from our hands holding the silver bowl
warm the air inside. Fleurs-de-lis winds the edge
of this wedding gift, and inside a single M—engraved
Edwardian script—identifies the family: McAlpine
a hundred years ago; Maughan decades later.
Now turning the M on its head, W stands for Wixon.

At Twelve

The summer Dad died
neighbors brought a three-layer cake
pink frosting flowers
Mother cut pieces   we took a bite
stopped   a taste like turpentine smells
Mother said *Oh they didn't know*
the cake cooled near wet paint
For school I wore hand-me-downs
brought by church women
one skirt and top fit perfectly
When a girl saw me she squealed
to someone by the lockers *That's mine*
Don't look I wasn't supposed to tell
Our doctor and dentist and orthodontist
told Mother *Don't worry*
you won't have to pay for your kids
Once a month I rode the Greyhound
an hour-and-a-half each way
to tighten wires   fit my retainer
I was always afraid
of losing my fare home
To keep taking piano lessons
Mother arranged I'd clean
the teacher's house
until I got scared of her husband
Then Mother said *You know enough now*
to teach yourself and the younger kids
when their fingers can reach an octave
We got grounded
after the Easter Massacre
when policemen ran across our alley
down the hill   lay flat aiming rifles
at the grain elevator   we crept
right behind them so we could see
who they were shooting at

Howard Street

It was a neighborhood where we played kick-the-can
under street lights that shone silver streaks when a can flew
through. In daylight, trikes circled single file until a car came by.

Neighbors kept discontent behind closed doors, except in summer
when anger flew out open windows. In Marin's house they took sides
silently, and when she moved we didn't know who took her.

Scrawny Mrs. Finch chain smoked and sipped from a glass
she refilled all day long. We never saw her go outside not even when
the car hit Joanie's dog and we stood beside him and cried.

Next door, Dr. Heald sat on the porch in his chair,
moaned or growled—the sounds he made when he came home
with a stroke. We ran fast past his house.

For our 4th of July parade, we fourteen kids decorated wagons,
pulled little ones, put on dress-ups, wove streamers in spokes
and around the necks of neighbor dogs. Two kids held sticks with a sign

saying GET WELL JACK, Jack in the hospital still broken by a car
and toboggan careening down C Street.
I was thirteen and wore a sparkly tiara and my blue one-piece

swimsuit, a MISS AMERICA banner tied across my flat chest.
I was ready for the big time—maybe the Rose Parade.
I practiced my wave until it was right.

My Brother, Another Life

He stands straight, looks like our father might have
at sixty: red hair turned white, freckles aged away.

At a lectern, he speaks in the voice of a man,
not the ten-year-old's faded in my memory.

He moves the laser and points to a word—maybe
a star with his name, or a cure he discovered,

or maybe he points at a photo of his new obsession:
Lucia's Blue larval stage 3.

He backs away, footage in reverse, and sits on a horse
loping over the pasture on that exhausted farm,

pleased, then startled when he's bucked
and plunges to the ground, limbs and head askew.

Back again—a man—no thought of the chapel too dark
for a boy's ashes, the oversized wreath of daisies

dyed yellow and blue for Boy Scout Troop #3.
His smile concludes his lecture as he steps off the podium.

What's Left Out of Chocolate Chip Cookies

When I chop pecans
I hold the memory
of two small boys
in Florida
where school wasn't required
where children worked
long days barefooted
dragging canvas bags
as long as they were tall
picking up wind-blown pecans

and blocks away my son
in the incubator
grasping for air
with insufficient lungs
the doctor saying
don't expect his ears or eyes
to work
don't expect his brain
to work
it's an institution for him
I wondered *someday*
will he gather pecans barefooted?

but now smells of melting
chocolate
brown sugar
toasting pecans
draw him to the kitchen
to ask *did you use eggs*
my chickens laid?

23

American Christmas

When my ancestors fled by boat, they writhed in storms
for months at sea. They left their baby born too early

to the cold Atlantic depths, dropped their old home-
country ways for a hardscrabble life.

Gathering with neighbors for celebrations, they learned
new tastes—leek pie, moussaka, borscht.

For generations, our family gave small gifts. Most hoped-for:
an orange in the toe of their Christmas stocking.

Some years we took in students for room and board.
Helga, Kaykay, Miep, and Hi-Soon,

whose sister was burned by napalm.
Each brought her family's dishes to the table.

Now we bake traditional Christmas cookies for neighbors:
Russian tea cakes, Armenian almond paste wreaths,

Scottish shortbread, Chinese hang-yen-bang with whole almonds
held in place by egg yolk wash. A favorite is Helga's recipe

for German gingerbread Santas with stiff white frosting
and red cinnamon eyes.

Small Words

A bright red hand severed at the wrist
hangs on a sign by her single-wide
she's pulled up and down I-5 for years.

Her clothesline strings crimson dirndls
and satin shirts to fly dry off Siletz Bay.
Inside, chairs stuffed tight squeeze in.

Two votives flicker a thumbtacked poster—
haloed Mary cradling Jesus on her lap—
askew from its last trip.

At one end, a bed stacked high with flowered
quilts and patterned pillows I saw long ago
in an old Dutch Masters painting.

We sit facing each other, knees touching.
Her finger follows my life lines.
She presses my palms together, kisses my thumbs.

Romany glides out like prayers, English falls cold, terse:
*slow down, you live too fast. You will soon meet
your life's true love. You will die at 84.*

Side Effects

Wherever we sit these days
is a waiting room.
—Alberto Ríos

We learn new meanings to simple words: host, fight,
harvest, graft, combining stem and cell.
New descriptions: spinning down, separating spongy bone,
changing shapes of chromosomes.

Two men arrive in Hazmat suits protected against
the eerie yellow chemical they deliver. Carefully they
hang the bag to flow drop by drop into her arm.

We wait and watch for new side effects that signal
poison is defiling in corrective ways, hear what chemo
doesn't kill radiation will, know both destroy inside out.

Ulcers eat her gums, her throat, mucous membranes
of her stomach, private parts. Her swollen tongue lolls raw.
Day and night, week by week, chemicals drip to crush,

to ease, to keep impairment at bay. Fluids flood in to wash
poison out but burns create their own solution, fill fingers,
toes, parts between—puff her tight as a vacuum seal.

Her skin blisters, stings with rash and by week six turns
to ash. She'll shed it like a snake—blackened armpits,
bottoms of her feet. New pink skin appears too tender to touch.

Twenty bruised nails slowly slough, grow back ridged
and rough—a topography of survival, of time yet to wait.
We know it will be months, even years.

Acknowledgments

With thanks to the editors of the following publications in which these poems first appeared:

"Metamorphosis" and "What's Left Out of Chocolate Chip Cookies." *Hubbub*. Portland, Oregon: Volume Twenty-nine, 2013.

"Fishing the Clearwater." *What the River Brings: Oregon River Poems*. Eugene, Oregon: Fae Press, 2012.

"Steptoe Butte." *Windfall: A Journal of Poetry of Place*. Portland, Oregon: Fall 2012, Volume 10, Number 1.

With thanks for faithful advice through many years from Ingrid Wendt, Sandra Scofield, Amy Miller, Amy MacLennan, and Vince Wixon.

Author's Biography

Patricia Wixon's poetry has appeared in many literary journals, including *Hubbub, Windfall, The Cresset,* and in several anthologies, most recently *A Ritual To Read Together: Poems in Conversation with William Stafford* (Woodley Press, 2013). *Airing the Sheets* (Finishing Line Press, 2011) is her previous chapbook. Since her retirement from public education, she has been a part-time researcher in the William Stafford Literary Archive producing ninety-seven CD recordings of Stafford's readings, workshops, and lectures. She and her husband Vince, longtime poetry editors for *Jefferson Monthly,* live in Ashland, Oregon, and received the 2014 Stewart H. Holbrook Literary Legacy Award.

www.ingramcontent.com/pod-product-compliance
Lightning Source LLC
Chambersburg PA
CBHW022349040426
42449CB00006B/795